lots of
Tongue
Twisters
for
kids

Also by Whee Winn

Lots of Jokes for Kids
Lots of Knock-Knock Jokes for Kids
The Super, Epic, Mega Joke Book for Kids
Lots of Christmas Jokes for Kids

lots of
Tongue
Twisters
for
kids

ZONDERkidz™

By Whee Winn

ZONDERKIDZ

Lots of Tongue Twisters for Kids
Copyright © 2019 by Zondervan

Requests for information should be addressed to:
Zonderkidz, 3900 *Sparks Dr. SE, Grand Rapids, Michigan 49546*

ISBN 978-0-310-76708-4 (softcover)

ISBN 978-0-310-76709-1 (ebook)

Interior design: Denise Froehlich

Printed in the United States of America

18 19 20 21 22 23 /LSC/ 10 9 8 7 6 5 4 3 2 1

Introduction

Dear Jokester,

Do you love words? Do you enjoy playing with words and how they sound and look? Then you are in luck!

You have in your hands a very special collection! It is a collection of tongue twisters that will amaze and amuse you and your friends and family. Read them quietly, read them aloud, and be sure to share. The tongue twisters and the unique bonus poems will entertain you and bring a smile to your face and maybe a little friendly frustration into your day.

Take a deep breath, do some vocal exercises, and dive in!

*He will yet fill your mouth with laughter
and your lips with shouts of joy.*

JOB 8:21

Contents

1

Wonderful Wordy Warm-Ups

A big blue bucket of blue blueberries.

He sees cheese.

Pooped purple pelicans.

Knapsack straps.

Red bulb, blue bulb.

Chester Cheetah chewed a chunk of cheap cheddar cheese.

Elegant elephants.

Penny's pretty pink piggy bank.

Great gray goats.

My mommy makes me muffins on Mondays.

Six short slow shepherds.

Ruth's red roof.

Please pay promptly.

Are our oars oak?

Much mashed mushrooms.

Betty better butter Brad's bread.

Three short sword sheaths.

Roland rode in a Rolls Royce.

If a dog chews shoes, whose shoes does he choose?

Mix, Miss, mix!

Four fine fresh fish for you.

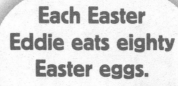

Six sticky skeletons.

He threw three free throws.

The blue bluebird blinks.

No shark shares swordfish steak.

Each Easter Eddie eats eighty Easter eggs.

She sells Swiss sweets.

Rolling red wagons.

Two toads, totally tired.

Scissors sizzle, thistles sizzle.

Inchworms itching.

A cheap ship trip.

Paul, please pause for proper applause.

White eraser? Right away, sir!

Draw drowsy ducks and drakes.

Thin sticks, thick bricks.

Crisp crusts crackle and crunch.

A pack of pesky pixies.

Big Ben blew big blue bubbles.

The glum groom grew glummer.

Silly sheep still asleep.

Kris Kringle carefully crunched candy canes.

Norse myths.

She shuffled so slowly.

People pledging plenty of pennies.

Roberta ran rings around the Roman ruins.

Sherry hates hairy states.

If he slipped, should she slip?

Yellow leather, yellow feather.

Hiccup teacup.

Nine nice night nymphs.

Keenly cleaning copper kettles.

Stupid superstition.

Pirates' private property.

Lonely lowland llamas are ladylike.

Three free tea trees.

The soldier's shoulder surely hurts.

Cheap sheep soup.

X-ray checks clear chests.

Kai's clay made Kay cry.

Bluebeard's blue bluebird.

Nine nimble noblemen nibbling nuts.

Where's Squire's spare wires?

Chrissy wishes for Christmas kisses.

Moose noshing much mush.

I saw Esau sitting on a seesaw. Esau, he saw me.

Valuable valley villas.

Blue glitter glue glues blue glitter.

Willie's really weary.

For real thrills, wear teal frills.

Mallory's hourly salary.

Six sharp smart sharks.

Tie twine to three tree twigs.

She said she'd sled.

"The bun is better buttered," Buffy muttered.

The sun shines on shop signs.

Slim Kim swims at the gym.

Plow power.

The torch scorched the porch.

Big bubble, bit trouble.

Two blue shoes for Tuesday blues.

Blair couldn't bear to care for the bare bear on her chair.

Wendy's window wouldn't win though.

Klaus's cat claws it in the closet.

Ten tennis men menace.

The girl swirls her pearly curls.

The goat boat totally floats over the moat.

The better sweater met wet cheddar.

Quaker equator, bakery baiter.

Red Reggie is ready.

Flowers float on the flowing moat.

Dirt girt Bert's shirt.

The funny monkey flung the spunky bunny.

The snuggly pug dug up an ugly slug.

Stab stable, scab cable.

Jumbled jungle.

The upright knight's trite plight.

The rabid rabbit ribbits.

Jen's in Lin's inn.

The loud, proud crowd bowed.

The warm storm swarmed the charmed farm.

Frugal funerals feature frozen fruit.

Marie flees the freed banshee.

Pierre's heir prepares a rare prayer.

Carefree Dee sees three trees.

The wee flea and wee bee agree to see the sea.

One fun nun has begun to run in the stunning sun.

The Madrid madman made Madam Maddie mad.

Samurai Samuel sambas.

Arrogant Ariel's Arabian arrow.

The moody moose moved the mousse.

Murphy Murray has mustard in his musty mustache.

Lauren's lawyer Lawrence launders laurels.

Sometimes, prime daytime mimes rhyme.

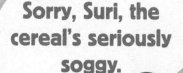

Sorry, Suri, the cereal's seriously soggy.

Polite Dwight's bright kite might ignite.

Claire's mare's fair hair's welfare.

Time for Titus Titan to tie his tight tie.

Lillian and Jillian will bill a million Brazilians.

Prim poodles prance and pretty pointers preen.

Plovers pluck a prince's purple parka.

Fran's frantic fan fans flavored flan.

Flynn flips a flooded flower float.

Penelope Penguin is penned in a pentagon pen.

Mable was able to stable the fabled sable.

Green grass grows great on gray ground.

Peppy people pepper peonies.

The foal will roll a coal bowl into the troll's hole.

Vain vultures veer over Venezuela.

The fishes flap and flip their fins.

Skylar skips and skates, sketches and skis.

Rick licked Nick's picnic chicken.

Chester's cheap chili cheddar cheese chicken.

The Zen hen has been in the wren's glen.

Thin twins, Lynn and Quinn, skinned their shins.

2

Marvelous Mouth-Muddlers

Nine nice night nurses nursing nicely.

"What ails Alex?" asks Alice.

A fat-free fruit float.

Shave a single shingle thin.

Four furious friends fought for the phone.

Six slippery snails slid slowly seaward.

A big, black-backed bumblebee.

Little Lillian lets lazy lizards lie along the lily pads.

Reading and writing are richly rewarding.

Baboon bamboo.

Six socks sit in a sink, soaking in soap suds.

An ape hates grape cakes.

A slimy snake slithered through the sandy Sahara.

Two tiny tigers take two taxis to town.

Red wedding ring.

Chocolate chip cookies in a copper coffee cup.

Freckle-faced Freddie fidgets.

Bulb-bowls.

Freshly-fried fat flying fish.

Betty and Bob brought back blue balloons from the big bazaar.

Gus goes by Blue Goose bus.

Craig Quinn's quick trip to Crabtree Creek.

Six sick sea serpents swam the seven seas.

Barbara Babcock blushes brilliantly.

Come kick six sticks quick.

The big black back brake broke badly.

Round and round the rugged rock the ragged rascal ran.

A missing mixture measure.

Brew a black blueberry brew.

Do thick tinkers think?

A cricket critic.

Nat the bat swats at Matt the gnat.

Seth's sharp spacesuit shrank.

Jack the jailbird jacked a jeep.

Bake big batches of bitter brown bread.

She had shoulder surgery.

Dean's Meals means deals.

A gentle judge judges justly.

Real rock wall.

Beautiful babbling brooks bubble between blossoming banks.

The fuzzy bee buzzed the buzzy busy beehive.

Crush grapes, grapes crush, crush grapes.

Upper roller, lower roller.

Quizzical quiz, kiss me quick.

Will Willow wear yellow?

Gail's maid mailed jade.

Plague-bearing prairie dogs.

Black background, brown background.

Sly Sam slurps Sally's soup.

A lump of red leather. A red leather lump.

Plain bun, plum bun.

Eve eagerly eating elegant Easter eggs.

The two-twenty-two train tore through the tunnel.

Such a shapeless sash!

Selfish sharks sell shut shellfish.

Argyle gargoyle.

Lily ladles little Letty's lentil soup.

Red whales weld rails.

Buy a black-backed bath brush.

Cooks cook
cupcakes quickly.

The clock's
lockbox rocks.

Bright blows the
broom on the brook's
bare brown banks.

Green glass globes glow greenly.

Smelly shoes and socks shock sisters.

Two tiny timid toads trying to trot to Tarrytown.

The tyke traded his kite for a trike.

We surely shall see the sun shine soon.

Alice asks for axes.

Reed Wade Road

Six sleek swans swam swiftly southwards.

Five frantic frogs fled from fifty fierce fishes.

Pre-shrunk silk shirts.

My cutlery cuts keenly and cleanly.

Stingy Steve sows stringy straw seeds.

The myth of Miss Muffet.

Triple pickle tickle trickle.

I saw a saw that could out-saw any other saw I ever saw.

Shriek, screak, squawk, and squeak.

Andrea and Andrew ate eight acidy apples accidentally.

Gus must bus just us to Russ.

The turtle is a hurdle that the bird'll hurdle.

The worst curse burst first.

A lamb trampled a scammer's lamp and scampered.

The pharaoh's narrow arrow and barrowed sparrow.

The liar squire hired a wire tire buyer.

The armadillo's pillow billows by the willow.

I cry, I dry my eye, I sigh.

Scarab scarves are scarce at Scarborough.

The dapper chap snapped,
and the happy rapper clapped.

The downcast class passed the vast grasses.

The mouse's spouse doused the louse's blouse.

Robert rebooted the rowboat robot.

Ross's boss's broths and sauces.

Jane's ankle is sprained. The sprain pain is Jane's bane.

Alas, a lass amasses brass spyglasses.

Drawling Paul hauls all small balls down the sprawling hall.

Belle fell and yelped for help. As Belle swelled, Elle yelled as well.

Thursday, the thug thwacked his thumb. Thus, the thug was thwarted.

The chow chow chose to chomp chocolate chowder and choked.

Brash Ashton trashes the ashen Shropshire shore.

Alex alerted his ally Alan of his alfalfa allergy.

Tall Saul's small doll falls and Saul bawls.

The ancient anchor of anxious Angus.

Caleb and Kayla's cayenne cake came.

The squirmy earthworm spurns to turn from the firm fern.

Kelli Keller's Celtic kelpie, Kelvin.

Anthony's anonymous answer annoyed Anna.

Albert Albany's albino albatross.

Sage Sarah says to sail to the saints' sanctuary.

The Japanese jaguar and jazzy jackal jabber.

The mutant mule's musical mural.

Nine kind canines find nine fine pines.

The blind swine's shined behind.

The fearful deer veered near the dreary pier.

The serious server's serene Serbian serpent.

Andrew and Angela's anticipated antiques.

3

Tough Tongue Twisters

A big bug bit the little beetle but the little beetle bit the big bug back.

Any noise annoys an oyster, but a noisy noise annoys an oyster more.

Clean clams crammed in clean cans.

Lesser leather never weathered wetter weather better.

Sherman shops at cheap chop suey shops.

The little addled adder added ads.

How many yaks could a yak pack pack if a yak pack could pack yaks?

A laurel-crowned clown.

Few free fruit flies fly from flames.

Ike ships ice chips in ice chips ships.

A canner can can anything that he can, but a canner can't can a can, can he?

Much whirling water makes the mill wheel work well.

On a lazy laser raiser lies a laser ray eraser.

You know New York, you need New York, you know you need unique New York.

Is a pleasant peasant's pheasant present?

Shelter for six sick scenic sightseers.

Bob bought a bleached blue-beaded blazer.

Suzie Seaword's fish-sauce shop sells unsifted thistles for thistle-sifters to sift.

The weird round ring wound around the wing.

Sascha sews slightly slashed sheets shut.

Abe and Babe will grab a grub from Greg.

Will Abe and Babe grab a grub from Greg?

If Abe and Babe will grab a grub from Greg, where's the grub from Greg Abe and Babe will grab?

Friendly fleas and fireflies.

The bleak breeze blights the bright blue blossom.

Jolly juggling jesters jauntily juggled jingling jacks.

Girl gargoyle, guy gargoyle.

Chop shops stock chops.

Miss Smith lisps as she talks and lists as she walks.

A good cook could cook as many cookies as a good cook who could cook cookies.

Old oily Ollie oils old oily autos.

Sheep shouldn't sleep in a shack. Sheep should sleep in a shed.

Sounding by sound is a sound method of sounding sounds.

Peter poked a poker at the piper, so the piper poked a pepper at Peter.

Rush the washing, Russel!

The bottom of the butter bucket is the buttered bucket bottom.

Two tried-and-true tridents.

The fickle finger of fate flips fat frogs flat.

Mix a box of mixed biscuits with a boxed biscuit mixer.

Six shy shavers sheared six shy sheep.

She sold six shabby sheared sheep on a ship.

Real weird rear wheels.

Barbara Babcock blushes brilliantly.

High-tech traveling tractor trailer truck tracker.

Tom threw Tim three thumbtacks.

Larry sent the latter a letter later.

The winkle ship sank, and the shrimp ship swam.

Ten tame tadpoles tucked tightly together in a thin tall tin.

Short soldiers should shoot sufficiently straight.

Quick kiss. Quicker kiss. Quickest kiss.

The ruddy widow really wants ripe watermelon and red roses when winter arrives.

Near an ear, a nearer ear, a nearly eerie ear.

The sheep each eat a peach and beets on the beach.

Ann Anteater ate Andy Alligator's apples, so angry Andy Alligator ate Ann Anteater's ants.

The cat catchers can't catch caught cats.

I see Isis's icy eyes.

A skunk sat on a stump and thunk the stump stunk, but the stump thunk the skunk stunk.

These tricky tongue twisters trip thrillingly off the tongue.

Listen to the local yokel yodel.

No nose knows like a gnome's nose knows.

Rory's lawn rake rarely rakes really right.

Clowns grow glowing crowns.

Flee from fog to fight flu fast.

The fuzzy bee buzzed the buzzy busy beehive.

Scared skunks scatter and skilled squirrels skitter.

Three fluffy feathers fell from Phoebe's flimsy fan.

Who washed Washington's white woolen underwear when Washington's washer woman went west?

Rex wrecks wet rocks.

If a black bug bleeds black blood, what color blood does a blue bug bleed?

So, this is the sushi chef.

Six shimmering sharks sharply striking shins.

The hare's ear heard ere the hare heeded.

Fred fed Ted bread and Ted fed Fred bread.

Shy Shelly says she shall sew sheets.

The teen green bean queen screams.

Can an active actor always actually act accurately?

Miss Smith's fish-sauce shop seldom sells shellfish.

The bland land band planned to handle sand candle stands.

The scarlet scarecrow scarcely scares.

The growing crow knows the glowing snow below.

It'll bristle a little in the brittle, chiseled hospital.

Vengeful Venetian vampires vie for vast velvet vaults.

Scruffy Scottish skunks scavenge scraps.

Get that frothy toffee coffee off me!

Smug Smith smudged smooth smocks.

The veiled jailer railed against the stale kale he failed to impale.

Starr stared, stammered, and stamped down the stained stairs.

That's a dapper, dappled apple sap wrapper.

Pale Dale unveils the upscale sail sale.

The branded man hands banned sand to the banded sand man.

Male quail trail flailing snail tails.

The ailing whale inhaled and wailed to no avail.

Randy ran a race that wound around a wood.

Of course, the hoarse Norse endorsed the coarse racehorse course.

Mossy sloths toss lost moths across frosty swaths.

When Ben spins the ten tin bins, then Ken grins.

Jane and Dane race down the main lane. Jane gains on Dane, but gains in vain.

Aghast, the last harassed steadfast outcast held fast.

The wizard scissored the lizard gizzard.

Ornery orangutans and orange orioles order Orlando orchids.

Lying Brian is buying Orion, the Hawaiian lion.

Food fumes fuel futile fools and furious future fugitives.

Furthermore, funky fungi and fuzzy fudge were found on furry, funny furniture.

Frivolous frogs frolicked on frozen fronds of frost.

The wife's strife is rife wildlife.

Alto alpacas almost always allude aloud.

Abashed Abby abandoned her abnormal abacus.

Embarrassed, Emily embraces emotional Emmet at the emperor's embassy.

Esther Rochester pestered Sylvester to test her zester.

Ethan's eaten at eastern Easter eateries.

Jasper Jansen's jagged jam jar.

Paige Paine pays the patient patriot to paint the pale pavement.

Tory and Corrie store Lori's inventory at Glory's quarry.

Shelby's shelf shelters Sheldon's shellacked seashells.

Jane Jade jails Jacob Jay and Jason James.

The muscly mustang munches multiple mulberry muffins.

The delightful white campsite's bright light frightened the spiteful sprite.

The sincere cashier cheered her teary peer.

The corgi corralled Courtney and her coral corduroy corset.

Their hare glared at the bear and dared to snare a pair of pears from the bear's lair.

4

Super Hard Head-Spinners

A tidy tiger tied a tie tighter to tidy her tiny tail.

Betty bought butter but the butter was bitter, so Betty bought better butter to make the bitter butter better.

Eleven benevolent elephants.

A big black bug bit a big black bear and made the big black bear bleed blood.

Does your sport shop stock short socks with spots?

Tim, the thin twin tinsmith.

Richard's wretched ratchet wrench.

Give Mr. Snipe's wife's knife a swipe.

An old scold sold a cold coal shovel.

Really leery, rarely Larry.

A cheeky chimp chucked cheap chocolate chips in the cheap chocolate chip shop.

Luther's sleuthing's useless truth.

Cows graze in groves on grass which grows in grooves in groves.

Kerry's chariot carries Harriet's hairy carrots.

Sarah saw a shot-silk sash shop full of shot-silk sashes as the sunshine shone on the side of the shot-silk sash shop.

That bloke's back bike brake-block broke.

A synonym for cinnamon is a cinnamon synonym.

Fran feeds fish fresh fish food.

Terry Teeter, a teeter-totter teacher, taught her daughter Tara to teeter-totter, but Tara Teeter didn't teeter-totter as Terry Teeter taught her.

Three thin thinkers thinking thick thoughtful thoughts.

If I assist a sister-assistant, will the sister's sister-assistant assist me?

Six thick thistle sticks. Six thick thistles stick.

The queen coined quick clipped quips.

Literally literary.

How much caramel can a canny cannonball cram in a camel if a canny cannonball can cram caramel in a camel?

Six sick slick slim sycamore saplings.

Pick a partner and practice passing, for if you pass proficiently, perhaps you'll play professionally.

Send toast to ten tense stout saints' ten tall tents.

Larry Hurley, a burly squirrel hurler, hurled a furry squirrel through a curly grill.

Nick knits Nixon's knickers.

A truly rural frugal ruler's mural.

Susan shineth shoes and socks; socks and shoes shine Susan. She ceased shining shoes and socks, for shoes and socks shock Susan.

No shipshape ships shop stocks shop-soiled shirts.

The ochre ogre ogled the poker.

Ingenious iguanas improvising an intricate impromptu tune on impossibly-impractical instruments.

Reece watched Ross switch his Irish wristwatch for a Swiss wristwatch.

The bootblack bought the black boot back.

Each sixth chick sat on a stick.

Billy Button bought a bunch of beautiful bananas. A bunch of beautiful bananas Billy Button bought. If Billy Button bought a bunch of beautiful bananas, where's the bunch of beautiful bananas Billy Button bought?

She should shun the shining sun.

Extinct insects' instincts.

Vincent vowed vengeance very vehemently.

Many an anemone sees an enemy anemone.

Ripe white wheat reapers reap ripe white wheat right.

If two witches were watching two watches, which witch would watch which watch?

Why may we melee, when we may waylay?

Sure the ship's shipshape, sir.

Twelve twins twirled twelve twigs.

Is this your sister's sixth zither, sir?

The British kitchen's skittish kitten.

Strict strong stringy Stephen Stretch slickly snared six sickly silky snakes.

Gobbling gargoyles gobbled gobbling goblins.

While we were walking, we were watching window washers wash Washington's windows with warm washing water.

Plymouth sleuths thwart Luther's slithering.

Rory the warrior and Roger the worrier were reared wrongly.

Sheena leads, Sheila needs.

How many cans can
a canner can if a
canner can can cans?
A canner can can
as many cans as a
canner can if a canner
can can cans.

Tragedy strategy.

Growing gray goats graze great green grassy groves.

Wally Winkle wriggles his white, wrinkled wig.

Our Joe wants to know if your Joe will lend our Joe your Joe's banjo. If your Joe won't lend our Joe your Joe's banjo, our Joe won't lend your Joe our Joe's banjo when our Joe has a banjo!

Cinnamon aluminum linoleum.

Three gray geese in the green grass grazing. Gray were the geese and green was the grass.

The great Greek grape growers grow great Greek grapes.

Which wristwatches are Swiss wristwatches?

Some shun sunshine, some shun shade.

The teller was a mellow, stellar, fellow cellar dweller.

Right writers write right rites. Left writers write left rites. Then left writers left left rites for right writers, and right writers left right rites for left writers. Now right writers write left rites and left writers write right rites.

Jill spilled quills down the hill. Jill was billed for the quills she spilled. Jill's quill bill will thrill the hill builders, and the billers who billed her.

Slick Nick flicked a thick brick. Sick Mick kicked the thick brick slick Nick flicked.

Skilled, shrunk shrimp skirmish and scrounge scrunched scraped scraps.

While Jon's long swan song was wrong, Ron's gong song did not belong. Don Prong's song's a con, so Don and Ron are gone, and Jon's long, wan swan song goes on.

A mink's hijinks: drink pink ink, wink, stink zinc sinks.

The frail fox balks as the hale ox blocks the locked mailbox.

Anna had a bandana. Hannah had a banana. Anna's bandana was a Montana bandana. Hannah's banana was a Havana banana from Diana's Banana Bonanza. Anna gave Savannah her bandana. Hannah gave Savannah her banana. Now Savannah has Anna's Montana bandana and Hannah's Diana's Banana Bonanza Havana banana.

Stuart Strong stopped at Stony Stream Storage on Steep Street to stow his strange steel stroller.

The shrieking she-shrike shrank, the shy she-shrew shuffled, and the shrub shuddered.

Caroline's carriage careened to the carnival.
Caroline came with caribou caramel, a
cardboard carnation, and a cardinal cardigan.

Genius Jenna's generous genie generally
generates genuine Geneva gentlemen.

Amazing Amber ambushed the amused
American ambassador among the ample
Amazon amulets.

Keen Keagan Keats keeps key
Kiev kiwis at the Kyoto kiosk.

**Logan loaded Loren's
loaned lotus onto the
local locomotive.**

The lonely lobster lost its lovely locket in the London lodge's lobby locker.

The antisocial android analyzed animals: an anchovy, an antelope's antlers, and an ant's antennae.

The Arctic archer and Arnold, the Arkansas armadillo, are arriving at the arena's artistic arch.

An Atlantic athlete atop an atrium attempted to attain the attic attendant's attention.

The apt apostles appeared to appraise an apartment apiece. The apostles approached and, apparently, approved and applauded.

Leah and Lisa lease a leafy Lima lemur.

Paprika the parakeet parades the papal paper parachute past papyrus parapets.

In the morning, Morgan mourns her mortal moray at Morris Morse's morbid morgue.

Mark Marlowe marched to Marcy Mars's marvelous market for marbles, maroon marshmallows, marmalade, and marsh marlin.

The dream drink dripped on the dream dress and the dream drum.

Sparkle and Spaghetti, spangled Spanish spaniels, sprint super spastically.

The panicking
penguin and
pensive pangolin
practice persnickety
Panamanian
penmanship.

William whispered to Willow, and Willow whistled while they whittled the whimsical white wicker.

I had drawn a swan I saw, a brown-down swan at dawn.

She shooed Stu, a shoe-chewer. Stu had chewed her two crew shoes too.

The scalded scalawag's scandalous scalp was scaled by a scaly scallop.

The twelfth fife, seventh viola, and fifth violin.

The Pennsylvanian's penchant is penny pennants and pendulum pendants.

Scheming schnauzers scent scholarly Schmidt schlepping schmaltzy schnitzel.

The prickly prince picked the principal's pinnacle pickle principles.

Snappy snakes snag snails. Snappers snare snacking snakes.

A rock hawk stalks a peacock in the stalks of phlox beside the loch's docks.

Pardon Parker Parr's particular partridge's partial parka.

The stalwart stallion stalked, stamped, stalled, and stampeded the stadium's staff.

The tale was titled "The Tattletale Toddler's Tattered Teeter-totter."

The withered wizard in the Blizzard River shivered.

The rambling ram rampaged round the ragged rabbit's ragweed and the raccoon's rare radishes.

The wonderful woman won a wonky woodchuck, wobbly wombat, wonderful wolverine, and woofing wolf.

Allie's Algerian alligator alliance was allotted all alluring alleyways.

Ere long, Ericka ran erring errands with her Airedale, Erin.

Robin robbed Robert Robespierre's robust robot's robe.

Paris Parrish has paranoid parents and a paralyzed Paraguay parrot.

The muddy mutt must munch mulchy mushrooms.

The cheap sheep's chop shop ships chips.

Three threatened thrushes thrashed through the threshold—thrillingly, they thrive.

His sister's six silver scissors sizzle.

The staid stag staggered to stagnate, staged stalagmites.

The scarred scorpion skewers the skittish skink's scant skeleton.

The Lincoln lynx links limp links of licorice.

Pandas pantomime pancakes and pansies for pantalooned panthers.

The whippet whimpered, and the whippoorwill whirled.

Time for Prime Rhymes (Poems and Limericks)

One-One was a racehorse.
Two-Two was one too.
When One-One won one race,
Two-Two won one too.

————————

A tutor who tooted the flute
Tried to tutor two tooters to toot.
Said the two to the tutor,
Is it harder to toot, or
To tutor two tooters to toot?

————————

I cannot bear to see a bear
Bear down upon a hare.
When bare of hair he strips the hare,
Right there I cry, "Forbear!"

————————

The owner of the Inside Inn
Was outside his Inside Inn
With his inside outside his Inside Inn.

Swan swam over the sea.
Swim, swan, swim!
Swan swam back again.
Well swum, swan!

———————

A certain young fellow named Beebee
Wished to marry a lady named Phoebe.
"But," he said, "I must see
What the minister's fee be
Before Phoebe be Phoebe Beebee."

———————

You've no need to light a night-light
On a light night like tonight,
For a night-light's light's a slight light,
And tonight's a night that's light.
When a night's light, like tonight's light,
It is really not quite right
To light night-lights with their slight lights
On a light night like tonight.

Pretty Kitty Creighton had a cotton batten cat.
The cotton batten cat was bitten by a rat.
The kitten that was bitten had a button for an eye,
and biting off the button made the cotton batten fly.

———————

Of all the felt I ever felt,
I never felt a piece of felt
which felt as fine as that felt felt,
when first I felt that felt hat's felt.

A tree toad loved a she-toad
Who lived up in a tree.
He was a two-toed tree toad
But a three-toed toad was she.
The two-toed tree toad tried to win
The three-toed she-toad's heart,
For the two-toed tree toad loved the ground
That the three-toed tree toad trod.
But the two-toed tree toad tried in vain.
He couldn't please her whim.
From her tree toad bower
With her three-toed power
The she-toad vetoed him.

————————

On mules we find two legs behind
And two we find before.
We stand behind before we find
What those behind be for.

Once upon a barren moor
There dwelt a bear, also a boar.
The bear could not bear the boar.
At last the bear could bear no more
Of that boar that bored him on the moor,
And so one morn he bored the boar.
That boar will bore the bear no more.

———————

Mr. See owned a saw,
And Mr. Soar owned a seesaw.
Now See's saw sawed Soar's seesaw
Before Soar saw See,
Which made Soar sore.
Had Soar seen See's saw
Before See sawed Soar's seesaw,
See's saw would not have sawed
Soar's seesaw.
So See's saw sawed Soar's seesaw.
But it was sad to see Soar so sore
Just because See's saw sawed
Soar's seesaw!

Lots of Jokes for Kids

Q: What do you get when you cross a parrot and a centipede?

A: A walkie-talkie!

Q: What kind of light did Noah install on the ark?

A: Floodlights

Introducing a collection of jokes that's hilarious, clean, and kid-friendly and includes everything from knock-knock jokes to Q&A jokes, tongue twisters, and a whole lot more. *Lots of Jokes for Kids* is certain to have every kid you know laughing out loud, snorting riotously, and generally gasping for air.

Lots of Knock-Knock Jokes for Kids

Whee Winn

Knock, knock.
Who's there?
Woo.
Woo who?
Don't get so excited, it's just a joke!

Knock, knock.
Who's there?
Anita.
Anita who?
Anita borrow a pencil.

New from Zonderkidz, here's a collection of knock-knock jokes that is both hilarious and wholesome. *Lots of Knock-Knock Jokes for Kids* is sure to send every kid you know to his knees in a breath-stealing, side-splitting, uncontrollable fit of giggles. It's that funny. And with more than 350 jokes, the laughs are sure to never quit.

This collection provides fun for the whole family and includes bonus Q& A jokes and riddles too!

Available in stores and online!

Super, Epic, Mega Joke Book for Kids

Whee Winn

The Super, Epic, Mega, Joke Book is just the thing for comedians and joke-lovers, young and old! Kid-friendly and fun, this collection of hundreds of jokes, riddles, tongue twisters, and more will keep everyone giggling for hours.

So, what's the funniest joke you'll find in this book?

Knock, knock.
Who's there?
Lena.
Lena who?
Lena little closer and I'll tell you!

Lots of Christmas Jokes for Kids

Whee Winn

Christmastime just got a whole lot merrier with *Lots of Christmas Jokes for Kids*. Over 250 hilarious, kid-friendly jokes and riddles will make the whole family laugh out loud!

Q: Why is it always cold at Christmastime?

A: Because Christmas is in Decembrrrr.

Q: Who delivers Christmas presents to cats?

A: Santa Claws!

Available in stores and online!

Read the sample jokes from
Lots of Jokes for Kids
ISBN: 9780310750574

What did one hat say to the other?
"Stay here, I'll go on ahead."

Why did the cookie cry?
Because his mom was a wafer so long.

What did the big bucket say to the little bucket?
"You look a little pail."

What kind of flower is on your face?
Tulips.

What do you call a bee having a bad hair day?
A Frisbee.

Why did the cookie go to the hospital?
He was feeling crumby.

What does a ghost wear in the rain?
Boooooots.

Read the sample of jokes from

Lots of Knock-Knock Jokes for Kids

ISBN: 9780310750628

Knock, knock.
Who's there?
Harry.
Harry who?
Harry up, it's cold out here!

Knock, knock.
Who's there?
William.
William who?
William, mind your own business!

Knock, knock.
Who's there?
Noah.
Noah who?
Noah good place we can get something to eat?

Knock, knock.
Who's there?
Dora.
Dora who?
Dora's locked. That's why I'm knocking!

Read this sample of jokes from
Lots of Christmas Jokes for Kids

ISBN: 9780310767107

What do you call Santa when he's broke?
Saint Nickel-less.

Which of Santa's reindeer is the most impolite?
Rude-olph.

How many presents can Santa fit in an empty sack?
Only one—after that it's not empty anymore.

What does Santa like to do in the garden?
Hoe, hoe, hoe.

Where does Santa put his suit after Christmas?
In the Claus-et.

Which side of a reindeer has the most fur?
The outside.

Read these sample jokes from
The Super, Epic, Mega Joke Book for Kids
ISBN: 9780310754794

What does a mommy squirrel say when her baby has been naughty?
You're nuttin' but trouble.

Which is the richest fish?
A goldfish.

What has a neck but no head?
A bottle.

Which knight wrote at the round table?
King Author.

Where do computers grow?
On Apple trees.

What did the big bucket say to the little bucket?
You look a little pail.

Why did the cookie go to the hospital?
He was feeling crumby.